Images of Modern America

THE MILWAUKEE CONNECTION
SPOKANE TO BUTTE

Highlighting the romance and ruggedness of the Western mountains, this 1950s Milwaukee Road advertisement promotes the newly equipped *Olympian Hiawatha*. (Author's collection.)

THE MILWAUKEE CONNECTION

SPOKANE TO BUTTE

Images of Modern America

DALE W. JONES

ARCADIA
PUBLISHING

Copyright © 2018 by Dale W. Jones
ISBN 978-1-4671-2880-3

Published by Arcadia Publishing
Charleston, South Carolina

Printed in the United States of America

Library of Congress Control Number: 2018932478

For all general information, please contact Arcadia Publishing:
Telephone 843-853-2070
Fax 843-853-0044
E-mail sales@arcadiapublishing.com
For customer service and orders:
Toll-Free 1-888-313-2665

Visit us on the Internet at www.arcadiapublishing.com

"We the willing, doing the impossible, for the unknowing, have done so much, for so long, we can now do anything, without nothing."
—Anonymous

CONTENTS

ACKNOWLEDGMENTS

Writing a book is not a singular undertaking. I will attempt to acknowledge all involved and apologize to those I may have missed. First, to my Dad and the fishing trips along the "North Fork" allowing me opportunities to spot a set of old Milwaukee boxcabs or a "Little Joe." There were several photographers who generously allowed me unhindered access to their collections. Jerry Quinn, the well-known railroad historian and master model railroad builder, gave me permission to peruse his extensive Pacific Northwest collection. Other photographers and researchers include Ed Lynch, who went "beyond the call of duty," providing scores of personal photographs and access to the collections of Doug Harrop and Wayne Monger; C.G. Heimerdinger Jr., who patiently scanned his priceless 1960s Ektachrome Pro 2.25-by-2.25-inch color slides of Deer Lodge and Butte; Rolland Meyers, who trusted the US Postal Service to deliver his St. Maries River Railroad slides; Thomas Hillebrant and Carl Sonner, with their Elk River branch images; Michael Sol and his superb historical Milwaukee Road website; Art Jacobsen for historical review; Gary Pember; Tom Burg; Rich Randall; Doug Cummings; Dan Schwanz; and Ken Secrest, who took an active interest in the project. Of course, a heartfelt thanks to my wife, Bonnie, for her unfailing support throughout the years; lastly, thanks to Stacia Bannerman and the staff at Arcadia Publishing and The History Press for providing me the opportunity to write *The Milwaukee Connection: Spokane to Butte*. The Milwaukee Road Lives!

INTRODUCTION

The Milwaukee Road story began quite inauspiciously. In November 1850, local dignitaries and railroad officials shared the excitement of riding in open-side freight cars five miles down the recently completely Milwaukee & Mississippi Railroad, built from Milwaukee and Wauwatosa, Wisconsin. The owners and promoters of this newly formed railway could have never imagined their little railroad would in time become one of the largest rail systems in the United States.

By 1872, the line stretched to Chicago, Illinois, and by the end of 1874, the then Milwaukee & St. Paul incorporated Chicago into its name, creating the Chicago, Milwaukee & St. Paul Railway, operating on 1,400 miles of mainline trackage. As the 1870s ended, the Milwaukee Road, known simply as "the Milwaukee," encompassed 3,775 miles of track, 425 locomotives, 300 passenger coaches, and 13,315 freight cars with total yearly net earnings exceeding $5.3 million. The railway's successful expansion in the 1880s did not go unnoticed by railroad barons of the day. As the 1890s approached, competition for lucrative West Coast and Pacific trade gained momentum. Railroad magnate James J. Hill of the Great Northern Railway and US Steel Company tycoon James P. Morgan looked to gain a monopoly on West Coast trade and sought to purchase the Milwaukee Road outright. The Standard Oil Company of J.D. Rockefeller and associates owned a majority of Milwaukee stock and tried to block a takeover of the Milwaukee by the Jim Hill/J.P. Morgan group. The battle ended when J.P. Morgan and James J. Hill acquired controlling interest of the Chicago, Burlington & Quincy Railroad (CB&Q) providing them the needed access into Chicago, thus competing with the Milwaukee Road. As the adverse effects of the CB&Q takeover unfolded, it was clear the Milwaukee would need to expand its properties to stay competitive with railroads already established to the Pacific coast.

In 1901, the financially stable Milwaukee Road had 6,596 miles of track, with its farthest northwest point at Evarts, North Dakota. In that year, the Milwaukee Road's president, A.J. Earling, sent engineers west to estimate the cost of building a line to the Pacific Northwest. After much deliberation, on November 28, 1905, the board of directors voted to commence construction to Tacoma and Seattle, Washington, allocating $45 million to complete the "Pacific Extension."

During the four years from 1906 through 1910, the little five-mile-long Milwaukee & Mississippi Railroad of 1850, now named the Chicago, Milwaukee & St. Paul Railway, grew from 7,000 to nearly 10,000 miles including the Pacific Extension and other branch feeder lines either built or acquired.

As the rails pushed into Montana, the railroad soon found steam operations in the Rocky Mountains difficult in frigid temperatures sometimes reaching 40 degrees below zero. In the early 1910s, electrical-powered locomotives (purists maintain that "locomotives" receive power from steam or diesel engines, whereas electric "motors" are directly supplied with energy from wire or a third rail) were becoming powerful and reliable enough to be used for long-haul rail service, reducing dependence on steam locomotives. At the same time, waterpower for generating electricity was developing in the Northwest, along with the copper mines and smelters of Butte and Anaconda, providing the means to support a reliable electrical delivery system. Considering potential future benefits, the Milwaukee Road's board of directors studied and approved plans to construct electrified rail operations in the Northwest. Perhaps not by coincidence, many of the high officials of the Milwaukee also stood to profit from the waterpower and copper properties needed to electrify the Pacific Extension.

By 1912, contracts were made for electric power, and in 1914, work began on 440 miles of electrification between Harlowton, Montana, and Avery, Idaho. On November 30, 1915, the Milwaukee's first electrically powered train took its inaugural run 112 miles from Three Forks to Deer Lodge, Montana. Ultimately, the extent of electrified track on the Pacific Extension totaled 656 miles through Montana, Idaho, and Washington, making it the largest such operation in the United States.

The benefits of electrification were undeniable. Consider this example: many electric locomotives were equipped with regenerative braking. Regenerative braking happens when electric motors are reversed from consuming electricity pulling tonnage upgrade to generating electricity as downhill train weight returns energy back into the locomotive. The railroad recovered about 12 percent of the power needed for uphill operations by trains during braking. After 60 years of service, some of the first electric motors purchased from 1915 to 1917 were still hauling freight until the end of electrification in 1974. Despite the apparent savings in operating expenses, the Milwaukee's financial condition had changed from being one of the most profitable Midwest railroads to a struggling transcontinental line. The final cost of the Pacific Extension from North Dakota to the West Coast escalated to $257 million, four times the original $45 million estimate, including the additional $22 million for the electrification system. The overextension of capital to build westward caused the company's debt and annual interest payments to mount. The Milwaukee began to encounter annual deficits beginning in 1921, and with the increasingly weak state of the company's finances, it was forced into bankruptcy on March 17, 1925. On March 31, 1927, the Chicago, Milwaukee & St. Paul and Pacific Railroad Company was organized to acquire the property of the previous Chicago, Milwaukee & St. Paul Railroad.

Perhaps due to the volatility of financial markets, advancing transportation technology, corporate mismanagement, or a combination of these circumstances, all electric operations were considered obsolete and discontinued on June 16, 1974. Pundits and "conspiracy theory" folks will continue to debate this part of the Milwaukee story for decades. In 1977, the Milwaukee Road went into bankruptcy for the last time; by March 1980, the railroad was forced to abandon all trackage west of Miles City, Montana. The identity of the Milwaukee Road slipped away as assets first bought by the Soo Line ultimately were absorbed by the Canadian Pacific Railroad. Today, all that is left of the Milwaukee Road's Pacific Extension are bits and pieces of track operating under independent owners, along with many miles of right-of-way converted to rail trails and local historical sites.

One

SPOKANE TO AVERY

During the late 1890s, the Union Pacific, Northern Pacific, and Great Northern Railways had a tight grip on nearly all freight traffic to the West Coast. When the Milwaukee entered the Northwest in 1909, it was compelled to duplicate hundreds of miles of track to reach the lucrative Pacific coast markets. Here, at Mica, Washington, SD40-2 No. 17 heads upgrade to Spokane. (Photograph by Jerry Quinn.)

The original 1907 Milwaukee Road survey located a more direct east-west alignment to the coast than its predecessors, bypassing Spokane about 40 miles south. The Milwaukee finally reached Spokane in 1913 after building north to Manito, Washington, connecting with the Oregon-Washington Railway and Navigation Company. The original Milwaukee rail yard was near downtown Spokane, but in 1954, the Milwaukee built a new 10-track classification yard and diesel locomotive maintenance facility at East Spokane. In these 1975 scenes, General Electric U25B No. 5003 at the engine house and a four-unit U-boat set led by U23B No. 4804 await assignments at East Spokane. (Both photographs by Jerry Quinn.)

The business car *Milwaukee*, in Union Pacific "Armour Yellow" and gray colors with switcher 627 in Milwaukee Road orange and black, appears freshly painted at East Spokane yard in May 1974. Built in 1948, the *Milwaukee* was used by senior railroad officials traveling the system to conduct business with customers or meet with employees. (Photograph by Jerry Quinn)

The Milwaukee Road and Union Pacific tracks paralleled each other along Trent Avenue near downtown Spokane. The Milwaukee assigned SW1200s to Spokane area locals; here, Milwaukee No. 614 runs the downtown local with a few cars from Centennial Mills while passing Union Pacific GP20 No. 492 on its way through Spokane. (Photograph by Wayne Monger)

In the 1970s, GE "U-boats" (General Electric class "U" for Universal, "B" for four-axle, and "C" as six-axle) were assigned to the Spokane region. Here, a combination of U23B and U25Bs pass through the horseshoe curve near Chester about eight miles east of Spokane. A joint track arrangement allowed the Milwaukee to share rails with the Union Pacific from Spokane to Manito before meeting with the Milwaukee mainline at Plummer, Idaho. The U-boat U28B No. 5001 creates a haze of diesel smoke while assaulting the continuous 1.4 to 1.7 percent eastward grade from Chester to Manito. (Photograph by Jerry Quinn)

One of the stipulations of the 1970 Burlington Northern Railroad merger gave the Milwaukee potential revenue opportunities; profits did not materialize, and the inevitable effects of deferred maintenance took their toll as roadbed deterioration continued and derailments became common. Following one of many accidents in the mid-1970s, an eastbound Milwaukee train powered by three SD40-2s wanders through unfamiliar Burlington Northern territory in Spokane Valley. (Photograph by Jerry Quinn.)

The late afternoon sun catches a five-unit string of Electric Motive Division (EMD) SD (six-axle Special Duty) locomotives near Plummer, Idaho, in November 1977. The SD40-2 No. 23 was one of 15 Locotrol master units; Locotrol was developed in the 1960s, giving front locomotives the ability to remotely control mid-train helpers for additional freight train horsepower and braking protection. (Photograph by Jerry Quinn.)

The SD40-2 series was considered the best-selling locomotive in EMD history. The reliability and versatility of the 3,000-horsepower 16-645-E3 V16 diesel made SD40-2s the industry standard from 1972 to 1984. Here, four "Dash-2s," as they were sometimes called, head toward the Highway 27 overpass near Mica, Washington. (Photograph by Jerry Quinn.)

Remnants of the Cold War are visible on Mica Peak in the background as three Milwaukee SD40-2s travel eastbound near Manito, Washington. In 1958, the Mica Peak Air Force Station operated as an early warning tracking location to identify enemy aircraft and direct Air Force interceptors. In the late 1970s, military radar capabilities were removed; FAA operations continue today. (Photograph by Jerry Quinn)

Plummer, Idaho, was pivotal to the development of the "Inland Empire." Although the Pacific Extension reached the area south of Spokane in 1908, by 1912, plans were being considered to build north to the Union Pacific at Manito, with connections to Spokane tapping the timber markets of Eastern Washington and Northern Idaho. Above, in September 1975, an eastbound Milwaukee Road SD40-2 No. 189 passes the atypical Plummer station; below, 34 years later in September 2009, the Union Pacific Railroad and locally owned St. Maries River Railroad swap cars at Plummer destined for Spokane or St. Maries. (Above, photograph by Jerry Quinn; below, photograph by Thomas Hillebrant.)

A variety of commodities from the region are illustrated in these photographs at Plummer, Idaho. The most profitable cargos were precious metals from the Union Pacific (UP) Railroad's Wallace branch near Kellogg and Wallace. The Milwaukee Road contributed lead, zinc, and timber from Metaline Falls on the Pend Oreille branch, with lumber and wood chips from mills at Plummer and Coeur d'Alene, and automobiles destined for Spokane. The Union Pacific abandoned its Tekoa, Washington, to Plummer freight line in 1955 to shorten the route to Spokane from the east. The UP then paid trackage rights on the Milwaukee north from Plummer, connecting back with its mainline at Manito. (Above, photograph by Wayne Monger; below, photograph by Doug Harrop, Ed Lynch collection.)

On a snowy January 1973 day, photographer Jerry Quinn hitched a cab ride on an eastbound freight train 100 miles from Malden, Washington, to Avery, Idaho. On the westward return trip to Malden, an eastbound train approaches a westbound freight near Calder, Idaho. The 8502 was one of four GE U36C locomotives purchased by the Milwaukee Road. (Photograph by Jerry Quinn.)

The two 3,000-horsepower EMD SD40-2s exiting the 2,559-foot Watts Tunnel, or Sorrento Tunnel, westbound will journey far away from the Milwaukee Road at Plummer in Northern Idaho. In 1985, the Ferrocarriles Nacionales de México bought dozens of former Milwaukee SD40-2s for use on Mexico's state-owned railway. (Photograph by Wayne Monger.)

The 2,200-foot Chatcolet Lake /Benewah Lake Trestle was a well-known photo opportunity on the Milwaukee mainline between Spokane and Butte, Montana. The wooden structure was built on a one-percent uphill grade east to west with a 10-foot elevation gain beginning midway. These two images were taken nearly 25 years apart; the photograph above catches the reflection of a Milwaukee Road westbound on Benewah Lake around 1979; below, in 2002, an osprey nest hangs over the westbound St. Maries River Railroad Plummer Turn. (Above, photograph by Ed Lynch; below, photograph by Thomas Hillebrant.)

The reds and golds of September 1979 accent the Milwaukee orange-and-black paint scheme on an EMD MP15AC, two GP9s ("GP" referred to EMD General Purpose, or "Geeps") and a bay-window caboose heading east on the Pedee viaduct to St. Maries and south down the Elk River branch to Clarkia, Idaho. In Milwaukee Road employee timetables, geographical south is listed as west. (Photograph by Ed Lynch.)

Between Plummer and St. Maries, the Milwaukee Road and Idaho State Route 5 parallel each other for 19 miles along the lower St. Joe River. In the late 1970s, Milwaukee SD40-2 No. 189 leads an eastbound freight out of the trees into open sunlight over the Highway 5 overcrossing. (Photograph by Jerry Quinn.)

The Milwaukee Road Elk River branch begins at the North First Street grade crossing in St. Maries. On a 98-degree afternoon on August 24, 1970, the switchman aligns GP9 No. 287 and the Elk River logger westbound (geographical south) to connections with the legendary Washington, Idaho & Montana Railway at Bovill, Idaho. (Photograph by Dale Jones.)

The St. Maries, Idaho, rail yard included several tracks for storage and assembling trains to and from Avery and the Elk River branch; there was also a modest locomotive repair facility and home base of right-of-way maintenance equipment. The St. Maries depot is of classic Milwaukee design and is now in use as headquarters for the St. Maries River Railroad. (Photograph by Jerry Quinn.)

The timber industry is a major contributor of revenue to a large portion of Northern Idaho. The Milwaukee built 475 "Skeleton" or pole log cars around the 1940s and converted many open gondolas to transport timber from forest to mills. Looking west from the Idaho Route 3 bridge in St. Maries, Milwaukee GP-9s shuffle log loads received from the Clarkia branch, which after sorting will be spotted back in the yard for delivery to local sawmills. Six miles west of St. Maries at Ramsdell was a unique transfer facility to off-load log cars directly into the St. Joe River. After being dumped into the river, the logs were corralled into large raft-like booms called brails and towed by tug to sawmills on Lake Coeur d'Alene. (Photograph by Ed Lynch.)

This idyllic scene at St. Maries yard on a late-winter morning in the 1970s is a typical representation of the Milwaukee Road in Northern Idaho. The 1950s home-built Milwaukee rib-side caboose No. 992071 rests on a roundhouse lead track with assorted boxcars next to an antiquated but usable sand tower. (Photograph by Jerry Quinn.)

The Milwaukee Road Elk River branch was constructed between 1909 and 1910 from St. Maries 72 miles south through Clarkia (pronounced Clark-ee) and Bovill, terminating at Elk River. The principle source of revenue was the timber resources of the region. Here, Milwaukee Road GP9s Nos. 282 and 285 work the line south of St. Maries. (Photograph by Ed Lynch.)

In the late 1970s, until the embargo of 1980, a few unscrupulous souvenir hunters took more than photographs while documenting the Milwaukee Road's final days in the West. Note the missing Milwaukee red-and-white locomotive heralds on the GP9s traveling to Clarkia from St. Maries with empty log cars at Santa, Idaho. (Photograph by Ed Lynch.)

In August 1970, three EMD GP9s—Nos. 287, 282, and 284—lead a westbound train out of St. Maries on the Elk River branch. Directly behind the locomotives is a lone home-built 40-foot gondola with 5.5-foot wood extensions designed to haul wood chips or sawmill waste called "hog fuel," used in firing lumber mill boilers. (Photograph by Dale Jones.)

On July 16, 1997, dozens of log flats with old-style friction bearing wheels create a cloud of smoke and squealing brakes on this eastbound (geographical north) train from the Clarkia log landing to St. Maries. This was taken near the Alder Creek siding at MP (milepost) 10.3, as the grade descent slows significantly after this point into town. (Photograph by Rolland Meyers.)

This pastoral scene of daisies at Fernwood, Idaho, is interrupted by three Milwaukee GP38-2s passing the depot with the westbound Bovill logger. The two boxcars behind the engines will be switched out at Garnet near Emerald Creek, with most of the log cars cut out at Clarkia before continuing to Bovill. (Photograph by Carl Sonner.)

In February 1996, the STMA line to Bovill received significant flood damage, taking the 15-mile segment between Bovill and Clarkia out of log train service. All log loading occurred at Clarkia after the February flood; here, in June 1996, St. Maries River Railroad No. 102 leads the Clarkia logger eastbound at Fernwood, Idaho. (Photograph by Thomas Hillebrant.)

The hills north of Clarkia are famous for Idaho gemstone garnets and non-gemstone industrial almandine garnets used in water filtration systems to infuse a refreshing mineral taste. In July 2002, STMA GP9 No. 102 switches log cars from the Emerald Creek siding continuing north (railroad west) to St. Maries. (Photograph by Rolland Meyers.)

In July 2001, white daisies bloom at the Potlatch Lumber reload log yard in Clarkia. The STMA transported wood products to the plywood mills and sawmills in St. Maries, the Medley Cedar Mill in Santa, and Scott paper chip plants in Tyson Creek. The STMA extended-vision caboose on the rear of this eastbound train has an interesting history. The railroad owned a vintage Milwaukee bay window (No. 995), like the one on page 22, swapping it for this former Burlington Northern extended cupola caboose that was repainted and renumbered as No. 997. (Photograph by Rolland Meyers.)

The photograph of this June 23, 1976, eastbound Bovill logger at Keeler was possible only on long summer afternoons. There is a cloud of blue brake smoke as three GP38-2s and a train of open gondola log cars ease down the approximately two-percent grade from the Sherwin, Idaho, summit following the St. Maries River into Clarkia and, ultimately, St. Maries. (Photograph by Carl Sonner.)

On June 21, 1976, this Bovill logger is eastbound by the timetable and just cresting the summit at Sherwin. The three-mile ascent on the south side of Sherwin Hill reaches a maximum grade of two percent and contains a significant amount of curvature for loaded log trains to overcome. (Photograph by Carl Sonner.)

Early on, the St. Maries River Railroad leased three locomotives from Morrison-Knudsen. The TE53-4E No. 5302 was cobbled together from parts of a Union Pacific U25B, a used 16-567B engine from a Baltimore & Ohio (B&O) F7A, and a custom nose and hood. This westbound train at Keeler, Idaho, has freight intended for delivery to the Burlington Northern at Bovill on August 11, 1980. (Photograph by Carl Sonner.)

After the March 1980 embargo, Potlatch Lumber Company purchased the former Milwaukee main line from St. Maries to Avery, including an interchange with Union Pacific at Plummer, Idaho, and the Elk River branch. Here, on July 24, 1995, STMA GP9 No. 101 and caboose No. 997 swap cars with the Burlington Northern Railroad at Bovill. (Photograph by Rolland Meyers.)

The Milwaukee Road mainline paralleled the St. Joe River 45 miles east from St. Maries to Avery. Much of the right-of-way closely followed the tranquil, flat-water river nicknamed "the Shadowy St. Joe." Near Calder, Idaho, two GP38-2s separate one of Milwaukee Road's four GE U36Cs. (Photograph by Jerry Quinn.)

Images of Milwaukee trains along the St. Joe River from St. Maries east to Avery are uncommon, as most railfans were pursuing opportunities to photograph the electrics over St. Paul Pass. This freight with four SD40-2s is westbound at the beginning of fast water near Herrick, Idaho. (Photograph by Wayne Monger.)

A westbound freight and four SD40-2s kick up dust during a meet with an eastbound train at Calder, Idaho. Railroad location names were frequently changed through the years to prevent train order mistakes; Calder, Idaho, was one such place. When the railroad reached the large meadow near the foot of Billy Goat Hill, Elk Prairie was the accepted name. At first, the Milwaukee stuck with that name, but confusion with similar names and a dislike of two-word station names led to the change to Calder. (Photograph by Wayne Monger.)

Two

AVERY

In 1894, Sam "49" Williams built his cabin at the confluence of the North Fork of the St. Joe and St. Joe Rivers. The Milwaukee made this flat piece of ground—now called Avery, Idaho—a division point in 1909, and later, the western terminal for the unique 440-mile electrification from Harlowton, Montana. Here, a Little Joe peeks through the Avery engine house. (Photograph by Jerry Quinn.)

Railfans had a lot of down time in Avery, as generally there were only about six trains a day, with many running in the dark. Taking a fishing trip up the North Fork helped the author and his father pass the time between trains. This view looking east from the Avery engine shops shows a typical June 1970 afternoon. (Photograph by Dale Jones.)

The 45-mile drive from St. Maries to Avery on ice-covered roads challenged many railfans; this unique view from the cab of an eastbound freight in January 1973 offers a panorama of the maintenance facilities at Avery. Electric powered rotary snowplow X900212 will require a heavier snowfall before being placed into service. (Photograph by Jerry Quinn.)

The Milwaukee was notorious for renumbering locomotives regularly, and these three SD40-2s at Avery from May 1974 are classic examples. The lead unit, built as 3010, later became 140; the next one is 179, renumbered 18; and last is 172, which apparently was not subject to any changes. (Photograph by Jerry Quinn.)

The narrow St. Joe River valley kept the Avery West yard in shadows much of the time. On the longest day of summer, June 20, 1970, the square face of E34A, part of the Class EF-5 four-unit E34 BDCA boxcab set, peeks out from behind the engine house. (Photograph by Dale Jones.)

The Tacoma Division was home base for many General Electric diesel locomotives. One employee stated that GE U-boats did not work out well in the Bitterroots as they leaked oil, ending up DIT (Dead in Train) to Tacoma for repair. Judging by this May 1974 black oil slick, U30B No. 5006 contributed to future oil cleanup at the Avery engine shops. (Photograph by Jerry Quinn.)

In August 1972, GP9s Nos. 327 and 329, with the Avery logger, are serviced at the Avery engine house before heading toward the short non-electrified log truck to rail reload facility east of town. In the 1950s, this spur was built to load homebuilt "skeleton" stake log flats or recycled gondolas with timber for the St. Maries sawmills. (Photograph by Jerry Quinn.)

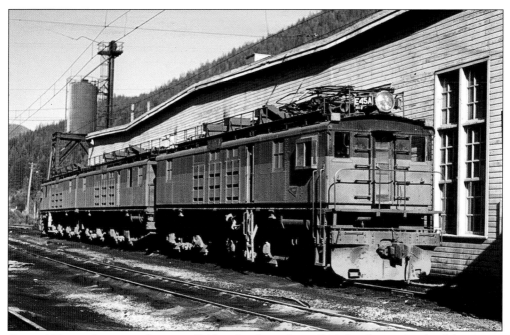

General Electric began production of Milwaukee boxcabs in 1914. On the north side of the engine house, this Class EF-2 three-unit E45ACB takes a break between helper assignments. Imagine this scene from the 1970s in black and white—it could have been recorded decades earlier. (Photograph by Jerry Quinn.)

On a quiet May 1974 day, two Little Joes sleep quietly at the Avery engine shop. The Joes were originally built to operate from both ends, but around 1964, one cab had the controls removed and windows covered over. (Photograph by Jerry Quinn.)

Many methods of clearing snow from railroad tracks have been developed, but Orange Jull improved on an 1860s rotary snowplow design later perfected by Leslie Brothers and manufactured by Cooke Locomotive Works from the 1880s through the 1950s. The Milwaukee rotary snowplow X900212 used the most common blade arrangement. Originally steam-powered, the plow was converted to operate from electric catenary or auxiliary diesel power. (Photograph by Robert Jones, author's collection.)

On a cold, blustery May 1974 day, a Milwaukee employee prepares to repair catenary on St. Paul Pass. This piece of equipment is a model railroader's delight. It appears the main body is an MT19A Fairmount "speeder," but note the details: specialized lift buckets, assorted ropes, the ubiquitous jerrycan, and a miscellany of tools. (Photograph by Jerry Quinn.)

The St. Joe River, or "Joe," originates in two drainages; the main branch begins, coincidently, at St. Joe Lake near the Montana border. The North Fork of the St. Joe River is exactly that—the north fork, or "Little Joe," as locals call it. The Milwaukee met the Little Joe and Loop Creek at Pearson; all tributaries joined together at Avery. Above is four-unit westbound train No. 201 meeting two-engine eastbound train No. 200 along the north bank of the St. Joe River at low water on September 23, 1979. The photograph below, from May 1974, looks east into Avery yard, with the St. Joe River in high water. (Above, photograph by Ed Lynch; below, photograph by Jerry Quinn.)

In 1951, the Milwaukee started retiring its aging boxcabs; by 1963, attrition was taking its toll as support frames weakened and electrical equipment became plagued by short circuits. There were only five boxcab freight motors still operational on the Rocky Mountain Division by January 1972. Here, at Avery in August 1972, the E45ACB set has less than a year remaining assisting trains over the mountain passes of Idaho and Montana. (Photograph by Jerry Quinn.)

In the background, Little Joe E74 helper has recently uncoupled from a westbound freight as crew members climb aboard a diesel powered SD40-2 continuing to the coast. On the main Avery depot track, the E79 was brought out of retirement to work until June 1974, when the last eastbound Joe-powered trains ran over St. Paul Pass. (Photograph by Jerry Quinn.)

In 1970, the combined resources of the mega-merger Burlington Northern consolidated services to shippers while creating competitive revenue opportunities for the Milwaukee Road; unfortunately, the Milwaukee was not able to garner enough business to remain profitable. Prior to the merger, deferred maintenance of the railroad's physical plant, aging locomotives, and dated electrical distribution system forced the Milwaukee into the inevitable decision to slash service. On this cold, rainy afternoon, the boy in the red raincoat could not know the historical significance of the day. On Saturday, April 27, 1974, the last 1916 Milwaukee Road boxcabs E34A, E45C, and E34B were towed west from Avery to a Tacoma scrapyard. Two months later, on June 15, 1974, the Milwaukee ended its mainline electrification. (Photograph by Dale Jones.)

How was the name Avery chosen? In early days, the location was referred to as "49 City," or "North Fork." It seems that Avery was named after the grandson of William Rockefeller, brother of J.D. Rockefeller, a longtime director of the Milwaukee Road. In June 1973, Little Joe E70 waits at the east end of the depot. (Photograph by Jerry Quinn.)

Considering the amount of snow and ice hanging off the nose of Little Joe E76, evidently it has not moved for a while. Perhaps there was a derailment in St. Paul Pass or some other delay. It appears the crew is readying the train to head east from the Avery depot on January 1973. (Photograph by Jerry Quinn.)

After electric operations shut down in 1974, St. Maries became the division point until the March 1980 abandonment. As traffic patterns changed, Avery slowly lost its significance, with unnecessary yard tracks gradually removed. Here, on September 23, 1979, an eastbound train led by SD40-2 No. 160 passes the Avery electric substation, which was demolished around 1987. (Photograph by Ed Lynch.)

Most right-of-way maintenance is scheduled during the long daylight of the summer months. This ballast train has been working along the North Fork before the snow flies. Boxcab Class EF-1 Nos. E45A-E45B, Milwaukee Road cupola caboose No. 990611, and a string of hopper cars rest briefly on this October 1973 afternoon at Avery yard. (Photograph by Jerry Quinn.)

The Milwaukee used only four different classes of electric motors in mainline service. The first were the General Electric boxcabs beginning in 1915, followed by five General Electric Bipolars with their horizontal tin-can appearance, publicized by Lionel toy trains in the 1920s. The third were 10 Westinghouse Quills built in 1919. The complicated quill-drive system gave a smooth ride, speed, and power, but also high maintenance costs and other persistent problems. The last units purchased were 5,500-horsepower 2-D+D-2 electric motors from General Electric. The Russian government ordered 12 custom electrics in 1948, but as east-west relations cooled, the Soviets did not buy the locomotives. The Milwaukee purchased all 12 motors for $1 million. No doubt alluding to Russian leader Joseph Stalin, employees called them "Joe Stalins" soon after arrival, and later "Little Joes." Westbound Little Joe E72 arrives on yard track three at Avery. (Author's collection.)

Here is a classic view of operations at Avery. The October 1973 afternoon sun creates a backdrop of mountain shadows while on the far right, employees bask in the sun near the house track. Center stage is E45A with a westbound ballast train as a Little Joe–powered westbound kicks up dust while descending St. Paul Pass. (Photograph by Jerry Quinn.)

In July 1971, the last rays of sunshine cast long shadows on a boxcab helper and Little Joe–powered Extra E76 West. Dispatchers were not fond of having trains pass on the hill, so there was a flurry of activity every time a couple of trains arrived at Avery. (Photograph by Jerry Quinn.)

The Milwaukee railroad tracks, North Fork, and St. Joe Rivers and road converged at Avery East yard. Here, westbound Little Joe E70 is exiting the North Fork canyon, and in the background is the main branch of the St. Joe River. In the foreground is the only road in or out of Avery. (Photograph by Jerry Quinn.)

Judging by the low angle of the morning sun and removal of all tracks except the mainline, this photograph at Avery East yard from September 1979 provides a glimpse of the last few months in the Rocky Mountains before total abandonment of lines west in March 1980. (Photograph by Ed Lynch.)

Three

THE NORTH FORK

This image captures the essence of railroading along the banks of the North Fork of the St. Joe River, including a clear blue sky and a westbound train with Little Joes crossing Big Dick Creek. Folklorists say "Big Dick" lived near here poling logs on the river; evidently, the trestle was named after him. (Photograph by Jerry Quinn.)

By late summer, the lack of water from snowpack and mountain springs has reduced the flow of the North Fork of the St. Joe River significantly; on this early August 1972 morning, westbound Little Joe E75 and three Dash-2s slowly enter Avery East yard at MP 1772.33 along the trickling North Fork. (Photograph by Jerry Quinn.)

Extra E75 West approaches Avery in the summer of 1972; the Little Joe will be uncoupled as the SD40-2s continue west. Avery was the major division point between the Idaho and Coast Divisions. All Rocky Mountain electric operations terminated at Avery, which was a crew change and layover stop with the time switch from Mountain to Pacific time. (Photograph by Jerry Quinn.)

Stream fishing in North Idaho is best in late spring or early summer; in June 1973, the crystal-clear waters of the North Fork bring together a perfect day of trout fishing and train watching. Trudging up the 1.7-percent grade near 49-Gulch, one Joe and three SD40-2s drag a 5,500-ton eastbound freight toward St. Paul Pass. (Photograph by Jerry Quinn.)

US Forest Service Road 456 headed up the east side of the North Fork on a tangent slightly above railroad grade. This August 1972 image shows the contrast in elevations between river, railroad right-of-way, and road, giving photographers an ideal spot to catch glimpses of westbound trains off St. Paul Pass. (Photograph by Jerry Quinn.)

A dusting of wet late-spring snow is a reminder that North Idaho winters do not give up easily. In this photograph from May 15, 1974, there is but one month left for electric operations on the Milwaukee Road. In the lead, Little Joes E72 and E73 assist an eastbound near Stetson. (Photograph by Jerry Quinn.)

The photographer's 300-mm telephoto lens foreshortens the distance between the train and highway bridge near Avery. The westbound Little Joe E74 with three diesels approaches block signals No. 209 at the east yard in October 1973. Milwaukee Road historian Stanley Johnson relates that during winter months, employees de-iced this switch with salt, inadvertently attracting deer to this location. (Photograph by Jerry Quinn.)

Active logging operations and subsequent truck traffic in the Northern Idaho mountains make meeting a log truck a bit frightening. The best way to gauge the distance of approaching traffic is by spotting the dust cloud above the road; note the haze from a passing vehicle on Road 456 below Tunnel 34, and a westbound freight. (Photograph by Jerry Quinn.)

From Avery north to St. Paul Pass, the road was at or below railway grade along the river; only near Stetson was it possible to photograph looking down to the right-of-way. Note the accumulation of old ties and other track maintenance debris thrown over the bank of the North Fork as a Little Joe and three SD40-2s head eastbound. (Photograph by Jerry Quinn.)

Examining a photograph closely can provide hints to time and place. Printed on this slide is the date October 1973. The Milwaukee ceased operating all Little Joes on June 15, 1974, so this date fits that timeframe. The railroad repaired portions of the track throughout St. Paul Pass in 1973, and new ties along the right-of-way indicate work has started. The most interesting detail are the ice-cooled refrigerator cars directly behind the Little Joe and locomotives. The last season the Milwaukee shipped Moses Lake onions and potatoes east was 1973. Trains iced at Othello, Washington, had only 18 hours to re-ice at Deer Lodge, Montana. All these details confirm the photograph is indeed from October 1973. (Photograph by Jerry Quinn.)

By all appearances, EMD SD40-2s Nos. 16 and 19 have just been washed at Tacoma. Unlike some railroad color nomenclature like "Omaha Orange" on the Great Northern Railway, Milwaukee's modern-day colors were just plain orange and black. This eastbound freight No. 200 is north of Avery near 49 Gulch in the North Fork canyon. (Photograph by Ed Lynch.)

This maintenance-of-way ballast train appears to be working south of the Stetson trestle near MP 1768 in October 1973. Milepost numbers were counted from Chicago; therefore, MP 1768 was 1,768 miles west of Chicago. Today, railroad mileage locations are marked as "CP," or control points, which remain constant after changes in track alignments. (Photograph by Jerry Quinn.)

The Little Joes were delivered in 1950 with a stylish orange and maroon paint scheme; after modifications to the motors in 1964, the electrics were slowly repainted into solid orange and black. These two Joes and a Geep are forming a haze of brake smoke through Stetson siding downgrade along the North Fork westward to Avery. (Jerry Quinn collection.)

While attacking the one-and-a-half grade just west of Stetson Tunnel, the internal combustion diesel engines of two headend SD40-2s growl as blue exhaust rises into a hazy September 1979 sky. Two Locotrol mid-train SD40-2s about halfway back assist this eastbound train up St. Paul Pass. (Photograph by Ed Lynch.)

These two images illustrate the height and length of the 515-foot Stetson viaduct. While traveling across this imposing structure near MP 1768, the Milwaukee moved from running on the east side of the North Fork valley to the west side. This change from east to west hillside exposure offered an opportunity to photograph trains in good sunlight at various times of day. Above, in June 1978, Doug Harrop climbed a steep hill looking north up the Little Joe as three SD40-2s crossed the canyon westward. Below, Milwaukee trains appear to loom out into the blue North Idaho summer sky while standing on the dusty road near the Forest Service Telichpah Campground. (Above, photograph by Doug Harrop, Ed Lynch collection; below, photograph by Jerry Quinn.)

The first General Electric boxcab motors were delivered between November 1915 and May 1917. The square profile of E45A reveals the mid-1910s vintage. Along the North Fork in October 1973, an Avery-bound train dumps ballast to stabilize the roadbed. Standard gauge rail spacing is 4 feet, 8.5 inches, based on early 1830s English railway measurements that are in turn traced back to Roman chariot roads. (Photograph by Jerry Quinn.)

During the 1970s, the Milwaukee was plagued by frequent derailments. Many factors contributed to the rash of accidents, including deferred maintenance of the right-of-way, equipment failure, or other circumstances—whatever the cause, this was one of many grain cars that ended up in the North Fork of the St. Joe River. (Photograph by Jerry Quinn.)

Four

ST. PAUL PASS EAST

In one of the few photographs taken from the cab of a Little Joe, this eastward view from 15 feet above the rails provides a cross-section of an average right-of-way along the St. Regis River through St. Paul Pass near Henderson, Montana. (Author's collection.)

In August 1910, fires devastated three million acres of timberland throughout the Rocky Mountain West. For many, the newly built Milwaukee Road through the Bitterroots became the only chance for survival. The photograph above shows a westbound near the scene of a miraculous escape at Falcon. A rescue train had gathered up everyone along the tracks but soon became surrounded by fire; the only safe place was inside Tunnel 27, which kept the fire and smoke at bay. Describing the ordeal, one survivor stated, "The roar of the fire was deafening and the heat terrible." Incredibly, 167 people survived. Below, two Joes with an eastbound freight cross the 850-foot Kelly Creek Trestle heading up the 1.7-percent grade to Roland. Note the silver snags left standing from the 1910 inferno. (Above, photograph by Dale Jones; below, photograph by Jerry Quinn.)

The railroad between Roland and Avery has been described as the most beautiful and yet most expensive two dozen miles of track on the Pacific Extension. The pass contained 16 tunnels and nine tall steel trestles, and involved moving thousands of cubic yards of excavated mountain hillsides. St. Paul Pass Tunnel No. 20 west portal (Roland) is in Idaho; the 8,771-foot tunnel peaks 14 feet higher in the middle before descending downgrade to East Portal in Montana. The slope inside the tunnel allows for drainage, and even today, water trickles from the ceiling—coats are recommended when riding the Hiawatha Trail. These images show eastbound trains in two seasons; the autumn colors seen above quickly change into snowy white, keeping Roland inaccessible for much of the year. (Both photographs by Jerry Quinn.)

Extra E21 West rolls through East Portal toward St. Paul Pass Tunnel on the final stretch of a nearly continuous 14-mile 1.7-percent uphill grade from Haugan, Montana. The gray of the timeworn maintenance buildings appears as dreary as the February 1973 sky. Halfway back in the train is boxcab set E34A, E45C, and E34B sandwiched between a string of empty flatcars. (Photograph by Jerry Quinn.)

The array of manual switches, colored lights, and old dial-face electric meters looks like a mad scientist's desk; they are, in fact, operating controls for the East Portal power substation. Other than a few system upgrades, the power grid built in 1914 was basically the same as this 1973 photograph. (Photograph by Jerry Quinn.)

Interstate 90 paralleled the Milwaukee tracks for about 30 miles from Taft to St. Regis, Montana. Three SD40-2s pull an *XL Special* container train westbound along the colorless waters of the St. Regis River near Saltese on a gray winter day in February 1980. (Photograph by Ed Lynch.)

Little Joes were built with the capability to run nearly 70 mph, but here, the blur of the E20 heading east is the result of pacing the train. This was one of the few locations where the railroad parallels Interstate 90 in the St. Regis River valley. (Photograph by Jerry Quinn.)

After the 1933 flood destroyed the Northern Pacific Railway's route over Lookout Pass from St. Regis to Wallace, Idaho, the Milwaukee and Northern Pacific shared the same rails from St. Regis to Haugan. In this 1970s photograph, Extra E79 West and another Joe kick up dust at the interchange where the Milwaukee and Northern Pacific parted ways. (Photograph by Jerry Quinn.)

The highlight of a successful railfanning trip in St. Paul Pass included a photograph of westbound freights led by two Little Joes in the late afternoon summer sun on the DD-170 bridge over the Clark Fork River at St. Regis, Montana. (Jerry Quinn collection.)

St. Regis had a connection between the Milwaukee Road and the Northern Pacific (Burlington Northern). This February 11, 1980, photograph shows the Interstate 90 bridge over the Clark Fork during construction and a Milwaukee eastbound crossing over the Burlington Northern (BN) line from Missoula to Paradise. Note the BN train in the background waiting on the siding that accessed the Milwaukee from the west. (Photograph by Ed Lynch.)

The waters of the Clark Fork River run muddy on a sunny April 1974 day as Little Joes E79 and E76 drag two loaded auto-racks of 1974 Ford Vans and 1974 Ford Torinos with a string of empty boxcars westbound near Alberton. Before side-panel covered auto-racks were developed, vehicles were placed near the head-end to discourage vandalism. (Photograph by Jerry Quinn.)

The Milwaukee followed the Clark Fork River (not to be confused with the Clarks Fork of the Yellowstone River drainage) 140 miles from St. Regis to Garrison. Hanging on the hillside near Tarkio, one Little Joe and three Dash-2s travel east above the river and old US Highway 10 near Cobden, Montana. (Photograph by Jerry Quinn.)

Two impressive bridges crisscrossed the Clark Fork River and US Highway 10 about six miles east of Alberton at Cyr, Montana. Both bridges were legendary locations amongst Milwaukee Road photographers; here, crossing Bridge DD-142, the pantographs of Little Joe E71 reach high into a blue April 1974 sky. (Photograph by Jerry Quinn.)

Alberton was one of seven division points on the Rocky Mountain Division stretching from Miles City, Montana, to Avery, Idaho; these two images provide a glimpse of activities around the Alberton depot. Above, in April 1974, a Class EF5 Little Joe E71, another Joe, and two Dash-2s with a westbound train wait to change crews. Below, on February 11, 1980, the wall clock reads 1:17 p.m., indicating that this was probably "first-trick," or the 8:00 a.m. to 4:00 p.m. day shift. The agent appears undisturbed while dictating train orders or other duties as the red diagonal Milwaukee herald on a GP-40 Class 30-ERS-4 peers in through the station window. (Above, photograph by Jerry Quinn; below, photograph by Ed Lynch.)

On the western divisions, the Milwaukee separated routes into about 100-mile subdivisions to organize personnel, set pay scales, and create maintenance schedules. Only two weeks before their last run in June 1974, two Little Joes hustle a westbound freight near Tunnel 17 just east of Alberton. (Photograph by Jerry Quinn.)

On Nine-Mile Curve east of Soudan, two Joes and two EMD diesels cross over US Highway 10 westbound. The Milwaukee Road spared no expense when constructing concrete abutments for bridges on lines west; a century later, many structures remain intact, reflecting confidence in building the Pacific Extension. (Photograph by Jerry Quinn.)

The Northern Pacific arrived in Missoula on the east side of the Clark Fork River, and the Milwaukee on the west bank; after leaving Missoula, both railroads reached St. Regis on opposite sides of the river. The Northern Pacific built up the west side of the Clark Fork, with the Milwaukee Road on the east side. Here was the dilemma: the tracks had to cross somewhere, and here, on a fine July 10, 1979 afternoon, eastbound Milwaukee SD40-2 No. 174 approaches the crossover at Huson/Lusk, built to direct the railroads to the correct side of the river. (Photograph by Doug Harrop, Ed Lynch collection.)

Railroad officials waffled many months before announcing the final day of electric operations; finally, June 15, 1974, was chosen. Milwaukee historians and railfans desperately took as many pictures as possible before all went silent. On June 8, 1974, photographer Jerry Quinn took this shot of an eastbound freight off the Higgins Street bridge in Missoula. (Photograph by Jerry Quinn.)

Little Joe E74 approaches block signal 80-0 east of Missoula. This signal was considered a three-aspect light with green on top, yellow at center, and red on the bottom. The number 80 signifies it is 80 miles west from the division point at Deer Lodge, Montana. (Jerry Quinn collection.)

The Milwaukee Road and Northern Pacific paralleled each other for 15 miles from Ravenna to Bearmouth. The section was named "the Racetrack," as two trains could race each other. Little Joes were geared to run up to 70 mph, and Amtrak SDP40F Nos. 580 and 578 were geared up to 94 mph— chances are neither was at top speed. (Photograph by Jerry Quinn Jr., Jerry Quinn collection.)

Almost one month before the last run of Little Joe E74, this eastbound train speeds through Bearmouth on a beautiful "sucker day" on May 18, 1974. Sucker days were picturesque summer days of Montana sunshine when folks were inclined to purchase real estate, failing to consider what the weather was like the rest of the year. (Photograph by Jerry Quinn.)

Three miles east of the Ravenna Substation along US Highway 10 (now Interstate 90) was the Beavertail Tunnel. This dramatic 300mm telephoto image looks straight through the darkness of 904-foot Tunnel 16 as Little Joe E74 approaches the west portal on June 7, 1974. The Northern Pacific and Milwaukee both had tunnels here just feet apart. In 1908, as the Milwaukee was building though the valley, a devastating flood collapsed the Northern Pacific tunnel, causing the NP to reroute traffic on the Milwaukee for six weeks while its right-of-way was repaired. (Photograph by Jerry Quinn.)

In the late 1970s, during the final days of operations on the Pacific Extension, the Milwaukee was dogged by many accidents. Above, a 200- or 250-ton International Brownhoist crane is cleaning up remnants of a derailment at Bearmouth as Burlington Northern train No. 85 led by SD40-2 No. 6383 slips by on a 10-mph slow order. (Photograph by Ed Lynch.)

The Milwaukee Road electrical infrastructure built in 1915 was fed by 100,000-volt, three-phase alternating current to Milwaukee substations, where voltage was reduced and converted into 3,000-volt direct current. This Montana Power substation at Drummond, Montana, supplies electricity not to the Milwaukee, but to local customers, as EF4 E74 silently heads east. (Photograph by Jerry Quinn.)

If this *Olympian Hiawatha* No. 15 (even numbers are eastbound, odd numbers are westbound) is on time at the Gold Creek No. 8 brick substation, Bipolar E4 is passing through on a warm summer afternoon. Sometime around 1959, the Bipolars ceased hauling the *Hiawatha* on electrified sections. (Jerry Quinn collection.)

After a major overhaul at the Tacoma, Washington, (Tide Flats) engine shops, Milwaukee SW1200 No. 623 is eastbound with two SD40-2s on July 8, 1979, near Garrison; the 623 will return to the Miles City yard assignment. The Butte, Anaconda & Pacific Railway (BA&P) No. 106 was on loan to the Milwaukee to relieve a recent power shortage. (Photograph by Ed Lynch.)

Five

DEER LODGE AND BUTTE

Deer Lodge was the main heavy repair shop for locomotives and the headquarters of the Milwaukee's Rocky Mountain Division. The engine shops performed steam engine repair, wrecked locomotive restoration, routine car repair, and major overhauls of the electric motors. The operating controls of the E50 boxcab changed little through 56 years of service from 1915 to 1971. (Jerry Quinn collection.)

Three classes of Milwaukee main-line electrics are pictured here, except the Quills, removed from service in 1957. Bipolar E4, repainted into Union Pacific passenger colors, was scrapped in 1962, with the boxcabs surviving until 1974. Today, Little Joe E70 is on display at Deer Lodge. (Photograph by C.G. Heimerdinger Jr.)

After "the wires came down" in 1974, Deer Lodge remained the center of diesel maintenance on the Milwaukee mainline. In July 1979, two Milwaukee SD40-2s and BA&P GP9 No. 106 are parked near the roundhouse. Locomotive No. 134 displays the standard orange and black; No. 148 is painted in the "Billboard" scheme, and the BA&P Geep wears modified 1957 colors. (Photograph by Ed Lynch.)

The Little Joes were delivered in May 1950 in the *Olympian Hiawatha*, or "Halloween" orange and maroon. Many Milwaukee aficionados consider the Brooks Stevens–designed colors the most good-looking of all Milwaukee Road paint schemes. The E79 rests beneath the sand tower in Deer Lodge around 1963. To the right, note the sand cars built from steam locomotive tenders. (Photograph by Bruce Black, Jerry Quinn collection.)

The boxcabs were reliable but not invincible; by the 1960s, many were showing heavy wear. To keep the fleet running, the Milwaukee started cannibalizing older excessively worn units. The E42A and sisters were assigned to the Coast Division but sent to Deer Lodge for salvage. (Photograph by Bruce Black, Jerry Quinn collection.)

Engine E70 was the first Little Joe to operate on the Milwaukee Road. The E70 was built by General Electric as one of an order of 12 electric motors originally intended for delivery to the Soviet Union. The unit was converted from Russian wide gauge to American standard gauge and delivered to Harlowton, Montana, in December 1948 for a four-month trial. During this period, the engine carried GE colors and the number GE-750. This locomotive was later renumbered E70. The photograph above shows E70 at Deer Lodge on Saturday, February 3, 1962; the image below was captured during its 1993 trip through town toward permanent display. (Above, photograph by C.G. Heimerdinger Jr.; below, photograph by Ed Lynch.)

A dark sky over the Deer Lodge shop indicates a Montana thunderstorm is on the way. The E78 was unique from other Little Joes, as engine E78 was seriously damaged in 1966 and rebuilt with EMD F7 cabs and vertical-slotted Farr Air–style grills on the sides. (Photograph by Jerry Quinn.)

Charles "C.G." Heimerdinger Jr. used Ektachrome Pro 2.25-by-2.25-inch color slide film to photograph the Milwaukee Road around Butte and Anaconda during the 1960s. The decades have produced a slight color shift, adding a warm patina to E74 on a cold February 3, 1961, morning in front of Deer Lodge depot. (Photograph by C.G. Heimerdinger Jr.)

The Milwaukee had six major classification yards on lines west: Harlowton, Butte, Deer Lodge, Spokane, Seattle, and Tacoma. Only Butte and Deer Lodge were regularly assigned electrically operated switchers. In 1917, General Electric built four steeplecab motors ultimately numbered E80 through E83. Here, the E80 works the Deer Lodge yard. (Photograph by C.G. Heimerdinger Jr.)

The Milwaukee was truly a railroad "that time forgot." Running side by side in Deer Lodge are locomotives built 55 years apart. When the electrically powered steeplecab was built in 1917, practical diesel-powered railroad engines did not exist. The Milwaukee SD40-2, built in 1972, is technologically years ahead of the 1910s-vintage E82. (Photograph by Jerry Quinn.)

The Milwaukee owned two Little Joes equipped with steam boilers: the E20 delivered in December 1950, and E21 in January 1951. Both hauled passenger trains on the Rocky Mountain Division until 1958 when modified for freight service. Here, one of the passenger Joes is steaming away on a bitter cold winter day in Deer Lodge. (Author's collection.)

In the late 1950s, the need to move freight more efficiently became a concern; three Little Joes in tandem would overload the electrical distribution system, and attaching additional non-helper boxcabs was not cost effective. It was found that adding one GP9 diesel booster increased tonnage capacity. On a warm 1965 summer day, two Little Joes and a Geep change crews at Deer Lodge before heading east. (Author's collection.)

Many things changed in the 15 years between these images, yet much remained the same. Both photographers were facing east toward the Morel substation, standing on the US Highway 10 (Interstate 90) bridge. The EF-5 four-unit boxcab set assembled in the 1950s developed about 6,680 horsepower, compared to the 11,250 from four EMD second-generation diesels built in the 1960s. Some similarities between the 1950s and 1970s are the high-tension power lines and some of the approximately 40,000 trolley poles needed for the Milwaukee electrification. (Above, photograph by C.G. Heimerdinger Jr.; below, photograph by Ed Lynch.)

On March 25, 1978, an eastbound freight near Morel grinds up the continuous .06 grade beginning about 10 miles in the distance at Sinclair (Racetrack). The frozen lake in the background is part of the 300-square-mile Anaconda Company Smelter Superfund cleanup site located at the southern end of the Deer Lodge Valley. (Photograph by Doug Harrop, Ed Lynch collection.)

Cruising downgrade westbound near Finlen, Little Joe E20 and three EMD diesels slip out of the Butte/Silver Bow mining district into Deer Lodge Valley. Since the 1860s, the region along the Continental Divide from Helena to Dillion has been the center of mining activity. (Author's collection.)

These two photographs are a last hurrah for EMD FP7A Milwaukee Road No. 97C. Both were taken on February 26, 1980; above at Galen, and below at Finlen. What happened to 97C takes a bit of detective work. It appears the locomotive continued west returning on one of the last cleanup trains from Tacoma on March 10, 1980. From there, 97C was bought and sold many times until early 1985, when overhauled and restored to service for the Maryland Midland Railway and later to the Steamtown National Historic Site. Its final resting place is undetermined. (Both photographs by Doug Harrop, Ed Lynch collection.)

Between Silver Bow and Finlen, three railroads and Silver Bow Creek share a narrow, basalt-lined canyon. High on the east slope, the Milwaukee westbound *XL Special* leads the way. Silver Bow Creek flows at center, while in the background, a Burlington Northern local heads west to Garrison. At far right is the old BA&P line. (Photograph by Ed Lynch.)

This real-life diorama imitates a well-detailed model railroad, with lifelike trees, perfect rockwork, and assorted lineside poles. The upper track has a train with an assortment of Milwaukee Road 50-foot boxcars; on the main track, Burlington Northern GP30 and GP35s cross a perfectly modeled girder bridge. This is in fact Durant Canyon on July 8, 1979. (Photograph by Ed Lynch.)

Photographer C.G. Heimerdinger Jr. remarked on this well-known image: "On November 11th, 1964 Tom Guildersleeve and I chased Little Joe 73 East from Deer Lodge towards Butte. At Dawson, which was near Butte, we found the E45A sitting in the siding and we secured this photograph. The Little Joe was moving at around sixty mph." (Photograph by C.G. Heimerdinger Jr.)

Milwaukee boxcabs were divided into four basic classes. The EF-1 was a two-unit freight motor; the EF-2, a three-unit set; EF-3s had three units with a cabless "bobtail" in the middle; and the EF-5s were a four-unit arrangement. Here, EF-5 boxcab E45ACDB heads across the Deer Lodge Valley near Khors, Montana, in November 1964. (Photograph by C.G. Heimerdinger Jr.)

A 1915 boxcab E42 sets out cars at Gold Creek on November 10, 1964, alongside a 1914-era Craftsman-style substation bungalow. One employee remembers these company homes being quite comfortable, especially in an era when neighbors were often living in tiny, one-room tar-paper shacks. (Photograph by C.G. Heimerdinger Jr.)

Peaks in the Anaconda-Pintler Wilderness loom above an eastbound freight leaving Butte on a trip toward Pipestone Pass. Milwaukee SD40-2 No. 17 was one of eight Locotrol master locomotives equipped to power unmanned mid-train "slave" or helper units. (Photograph by Doug Harrop, Ed Lynch collection.)

Butte hosted two Milwaukee Road passenger locations: the historic 1910s station near Uptown Butte, now home to KXLF-TV, and the smaller, more compact 1950s depot at the foot of Josette Avenue. Little Joe E75 heads west on June 24, 1970, from the non-passenger station—the Butte yard office. (Photograph by Dale Jones.)

On the outskirts of Butte near Newcomb, the late-afternoon glare hides the Little Joe number board, but its identity is revealed by the unique stainless-steel side grills and revamped F7 diesel cab. Clearly, this is engine E78, leading an eastbound freight toward Pipestone Pass. (Photograph by Jerry Quinn.)

This dramatic telephoto image from June 1974 finds five of the twelve Milwaukee Little Joes in one photograph. In the distance, two Joes head east through Alloy next to the BA&P tracks. The two Joes and two diesels deadhead an EF-5 and SW1200 switcher to Deer Lodge for repair. (Photograph by Jerry Quinn.)

On a ballasted roadbed that looks remarkably well maintained for the late 1970s, two SD40-2s drift downgrade near Newcomb, Montana, on a rainy 1979 day. This image clearly shows the creosoted stubs inserted to stabilize the original cedar trolley poles as age and rot took their toll. (Photograph by Ed Lynch.)

The Milwaukee conquered five mountain ranges on the Pacific Extension, including the Belts and the Bitterroots in Montana, and the Saddle and Cascade Mountains in Washington, but the principal hurdle was the Continental Divide in Montana. On July 8, 1979, Milwaukee Road SD40-2 No. 148 is perfectly framed between catenary goalposts near Newcomb after beginning the assault up the 30-mile passage across the "Great Divide" over Pipestone Pass. The scars on the hillside in the background are Northern Pacific's Homestake Pass. Trailing behind the Milwaukee units is a leased BA&P GP9 headed for switching duty in Harlowton, also known as "Harlo." (Photograph by Ed Lynch.)

At Newcomb, Montana, the six locomotives on this westbound train illustrate the considerable horsepower needed to move freight through Pipestone Pass. Note the damaged crossties in front of the engines and shredded timbers, suggesting a train recently went "on the ground," revealing the deteriorated condition of the right-of-way during the late 1970s. (Photograph by Ed Lynch.)

The four-unit EF-5 class boxcabs consisted of A and B with full controls and two bobtail, or chopped cabless, and C and D middle units. The comparisons are clearly seen here as E34ACDB crosses the 590-foot Blacktail viaduct in Pipestone Pass on November 12, 1964. (Photograph by C.G. Heimerdinger Jr.)

The Janney Substation No. 6, located halfway up the west slope of the Rockies between Butte and the summit of Pipestone Pass, delivered power for electric locomotives. After June 1974, overhead wires no longer supplied electricity for Milwaukee trains on lines west. On March 25, 1978, all energy was supplied by 3,000-horsepower internal combustion SD40-2 diesel electric locomotives. (Photograph by Doug Harrop, Ed Lynch collection.)

On March 25, 1978, photographer Doug Harrop captured four SD40-2s on the westbound *XL Special* freight No. 261. The long, looping 155-degree horseshoe curve through this sparse region of Montana between Vendome and Cedric clearly illustrates why the Milwaukee Road could not produce enough revenue to support the Pacific Extension. (Photograph by Doug Harrop, Ed Lynch collection.)

Six

BUTTE, ANACONDA & PACIFIC RAILWAY

The Butte, Anaconda & Pacific Railway short line was founded in 1892 primarily to haul copper ore from the mines in Butte to the smelter in Anaconda. In 1913, the railroad was the first predominantly freight line in the nation to electrify. Here, boxcabs Nos. 48 and 46 pass through the large smelter on February 2, 1962. (Photograph by C.G. Heimerdinger Jr.)

The BA&P eventually owned a total of 28 General Electric boxcab units: 26 for freight and 2 for passenger service, built from 1913 to 1917. In February 1962, double-unit Nos. 46 and 48 were considered a 160-ton freight locomotive capable of giving a continuous sustained output of 2,100 horsepower. (Photograph by C.G. Heimerdinger Jr.)

BA&P engine No. 66 was one of two motors built in 1913 for passenger service. Passenger train ridership declined during the 20th century, and Nos. 65 and 66 were re-geared for freight service. Here, in 1962, No. 66 is transporting industrial chemicals inside the Washoe smelter at Anaconda. (Photograph by C.G. Heimerdinger Jr.)

In the late 1950s, the BA&P's aging electrical system required upgrading to remain profitable versus total dieselization. Ultimately, new ore cars, an electric substation, and two new specially designed 2,480-horsepower, 125-ton electric locomotives were purchased in 1957. Nos. 201 and 202 switch the Anaconda smelter yard on February 2, 1962. (Photograph by C.G. Heimerdinger Jr.)

In February 1962, at the Anaconda yard, one of three 40-ton tractor trucks is attached to motor No. 66, increasing the horsepower to a 120-ton six-axle unit capable of handling much heavier trains but at a slightly lower speed. One of the 0-4-4-0 boxcabs (No. 47) and "slug" T-1 are preserved at the World Mining Museum in Butte. (Photograph by C.G. Heimerdinger Jr.)

Line car M-10 was an eight-wheel, self-propelled unit built in 1925. The work platform on top of the car would be raised or lowered pneumatically for access to the overhead, and could carry enough men and equipment to perform most routine maintenance. The M-10 operated for the entire life of electrification and is presently on display in Butte. (Photograph by C.G. Heimerdinger Jr.)

Trains from the Stuart branch near Anaconda would deliver cars to the small yard below the Neversweat, Anaconda, and St. Lawrence Mines in Butte, where pulverized rock would be mixed with water and pumped into mining stopes to stabilize the hillsides. (Photograph by C.G. Heimerdinger Jr.)

In November 1964, BA&P Nos. 57 and 48 move a few loads of "slime," or waste rock mixed with water, along Virginia Street near the Little Mina Mine in Uptown Butte. The houses in the background, built around 1903, are part of Butte's historic mining heritage. (Photograph by C.G. Heimerdinger Jr.)

This November 11, 1964, night scene of BA&P engine No. 57 arriving at Rocker is remarkable in both content and composition. Reminiscent of a classic O. Winston Link black-and-white image, this color photograph was taken without a flash. (Photograph by T.H. Guildersleeve, C.G. Heimerdinger Jr. collection.)

The BA&P GP38-2 No. 109 leads a string of ore cars eastward to Butte near Rocker. The 109 is somewhat famous for playing a bit part in the 1985 Andrei Konchalovsky film *Runaway Train* starring Jon Voight. The movie is based on two escaped convicts and a female railway worker finding themselves trapped on a train with no brakes and nobody driving. Today, the unit still works for the Alaska Railway. (Photograph by Ed Lynch.)

The BA&P electric operations ceased in mid-1967, and the boxcabs were stored until scraped around 1973. The two custom GE 125-ton motors were sold for parts and scrapped in 1977. This scene from the 1950s at Rocker closes the chapter on the Butte, Anaconda & Pacific Railway. (Photograph by Sanford Goodrick, Ed Lynch collection.)

Why does the Milwaukee Road in the West appeal to so many people? One railroader stated, "The Milwaukee Road was the longest-running single line of railroad, traveling 2,700 miles from Chicago north to Minneapolis and westward to Seattle and Tacoma." Another reason is that it is just no more. This Johnny-come-lately faced and conquered the vast spaces of Montana and the Idaho mountains, embraced the emerging science of electric railroading, built massive earthworks, viaducts, tunnels, switchyards, and terminals, and vanished in less than 75 years. This 1970s photograph of a Little Joe sitting at the engine shops in Avery is proof that the Milwaukee Road lives on. (Photograph by Jerry Quinn.)

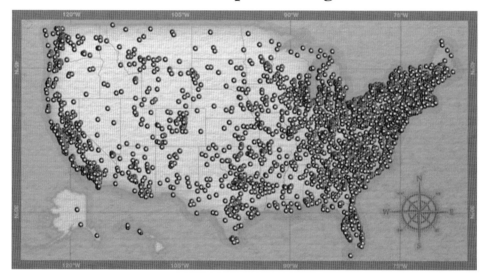